The BEATLES
Colouring Book

igloobooks

igloobooks

Published in 2023
First published in the UK by Igloo Books Ltd
An imprint of Igloo Books Ltd
Cottage Farm, NN6 0BJ, UK
Owned by Bonnier Books
Sveavägen 56, Stockholm, Sweden
www.igloobooks.com

Copyright © 2020 Igloo Books Ltd

All rights reserved. No part of this publication may be reproduced or transmitted in any form or by any means, electronic, or mechanical, including photocopying, recording, or by any information storage and retrieval system, without permission in writing from the publisher.

0723 005
2 4 6 8 10 9 7 5 3
ISBN 978-1-80022-505-3

Illustrated by Ceej Rowland

Designed by Jess Brown
Edited by Natalie Graham

Printed and manufactured in China

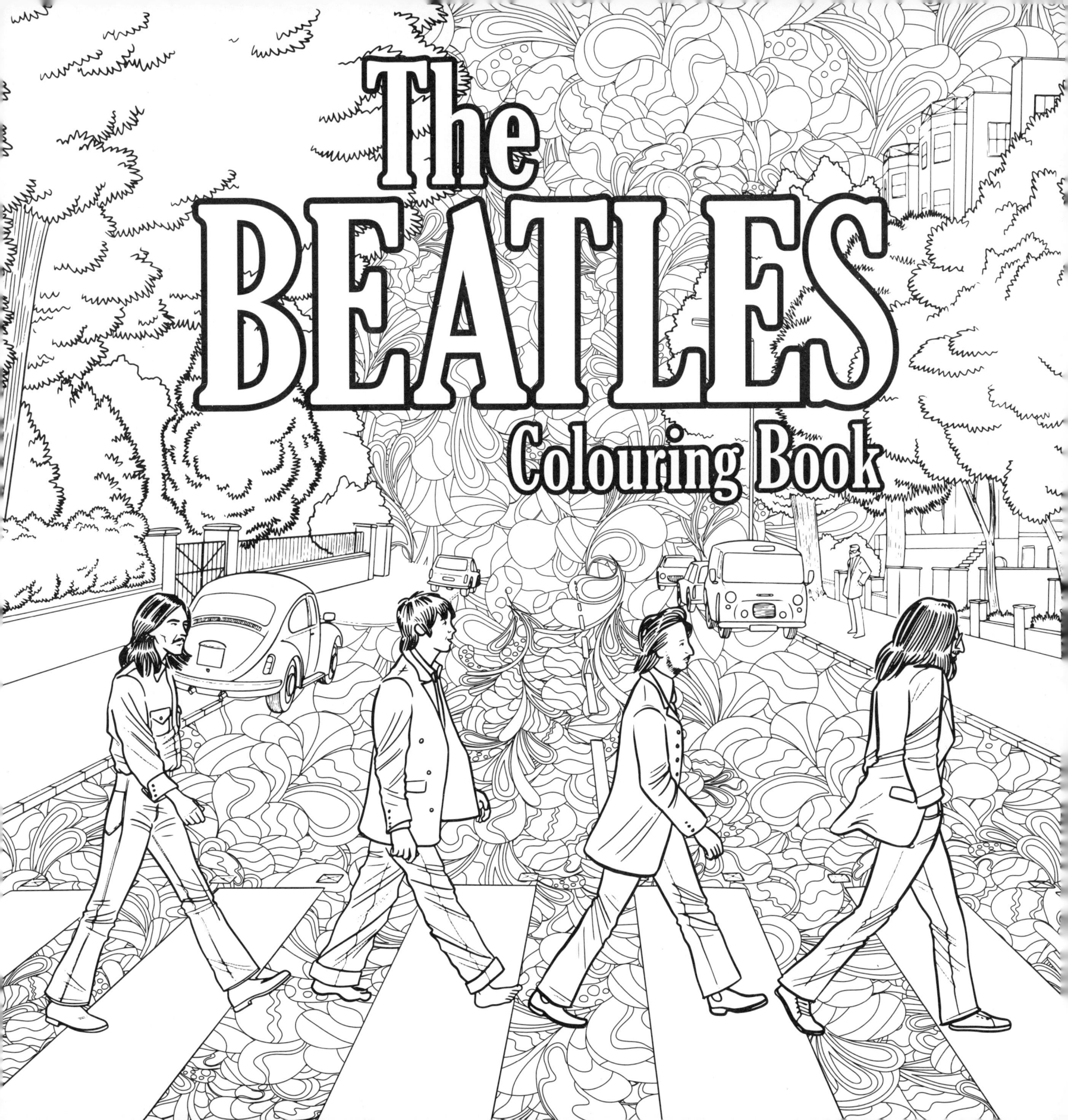

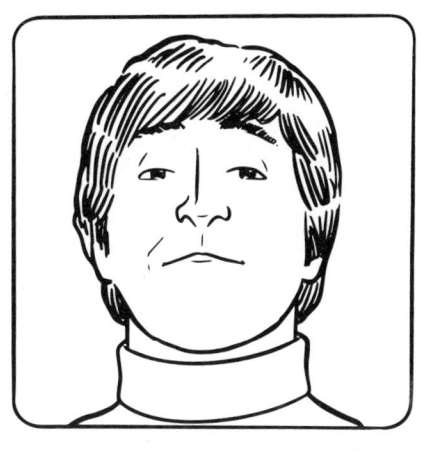

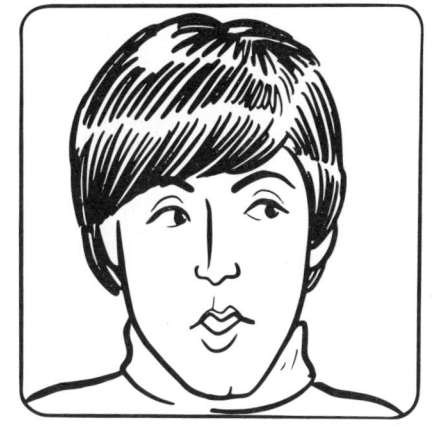

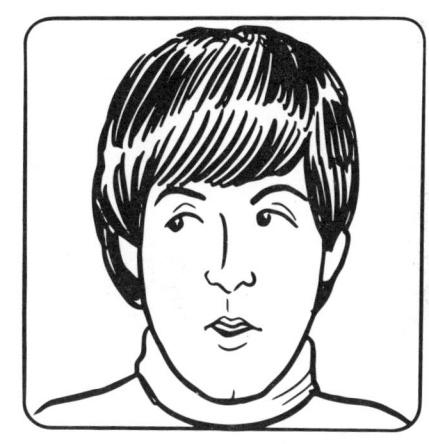

THE BEATLES
HELP!

The BEATLES

№ 0485863